T0083467

As Long as Trees
Take Root
in the Earth

THE AFRICA LIST

ALAIN
MABANCKOU

*As Long as Trees
Take Root
in the Earth*

AND OTHER POEMS

TRANSLATED BY NANCY NAOMI CARLSON

LONDON NEW YORK CALCUTTA

This project was supported in part by a translation fellowship
from the National Endowment for the Arts

www.bibliofrance.in

The work is published with the support of the Publication
Assistance Programmes of the Institut français

Seagull Books, 2021

Originally published as
Quand le coq annoncera l'aube d'un autre jour . . .
© L'Harmattan, 2000

Tant que les arbres s'enracineront dans la terre
© Mémoire d'encrier, 2003

An Open Letter to Those Who Are Killing Poetry © Alain Mabanckou, 2021

First published in English translation by Seagull Books, 2021
English translation and Foreword © Nancy Naomi Carlson, 2021

ISBN   978 0 8574 2 877 6

British Library Cataloguing-in-Publication Data
A catalogue record for this book is available from the British Library

Typeset by Seagull Books, Calcutta, India
Printed and bound by Versa Press, East Peoria, Illinois, USA

Contents

Translator's Foreword

Alain Mabanckou is no stranger to controversy, speaking his mind whenever he believes something needs to be said. Whether deploring the civil wars that have plagued his homeland or denouncing its president for revising the constitution to prolong a decades-long presidency, Mabanckou's urgent and uncompromising voice can be heard across the globe. Steadfast in his convictions, he even turned down an invitation from President Emmanuel Macron to participate in an initiative to promote the French language around the world, stating in an open letter that the language was not in jeopardy at all. Rather, it was being used to justify propping up corrupt African dictators. In 'An Open Letter to Those Who are Killing Poetry', included in this collection, Mabanckou takes aim at the 'literary establishment' in Africa and the cronyism that has infiltrated the French publishing industry.

For his provocative themes and literary merit, Mabanckou's work has garnered a multitude of awards, beginning in 1995, when his first poetry collection won the Prix de la Société des Poètes Français. Best known for his prose, which has been translated into close to twenty languages, including Catalan, English, Hebrew, Korean, Polish and Spanish, he was twice shortlisted for the Man Booker International Prize and been described by the *Guardian* as 'one of Africa's greatest writers.' Nobel Prize winner Jean-Marie Gustave Le Clézio stated, 'What captures our attention and moves us is his perspective on the madness and contradictions of postcolonial society.'

As Long as Trees Take Root in the Earth and Other Poems represents the first time any of Mabanckou's poetry has been translated into English, and contains the following two critically acclaimed full-length volumes: *Quand le coq annoncera l'aube d'un autre jour . . .* [When the Rooster Announces the Dawn of Another Day . . . ; first published in 2000]; and *Tant que les arbres s'enracineront dans la terre* [As Long as Trees Take Root in the Earth; 2003], followed by the essay referenced earlier. Mabanckou's poetry collections were well received when they first appeared, buoyed by prefaces by literary luminaries such as Jacques Chevrier, who praised Mabanckou's 'deep sense of what it means to be human'.

Stylistically, the poems in these two books, while remaining fairly accessible, demonstrate linguistic experimentation, including little punctuation and the lack of titles. Most are on the short side but all are intensely moving—especially the poems about Mabanckou's late mother. Others, also compact, make use of playful and ironic language that packs a punch. A subtle kind of music runs through the French texts, surfacing frequently in sound and rhythmic patterns, as well as silences. The challenge for me was to honour the original music. For example, in the first stanza of 'in this ancestral land', a music-themed poem, the French contains some understated assonance, as follows: 'cette' / 'terre'; 'bêcher' / 'détournées' / 'desertées' / 'barbelés'; some subtle *b*-alliteration ('l'embryon' / 'bêcher'); *l*-alliteration ('leur' / 'lit') and *v*-alliteration ('voix' / 's'élèvent').

> dans cette terre d'origine
> il y a l'embryon à bêcher
> le ramage des oiseaux de septembre
> les rivières détournées de leur lit
> les plantations désertées
> les fils barbelés autour des voix qui s'élèvent

I was able to capture some of this music in my translation, making use of assonance ('land'/ 'plant'), consonance ('**bird**s'/ 'di**ver**ted'/ 'de**ser**ted'/ '**cir**cling') and z-alliteration ('song**s**'/ 'bird**s**'/ 'river**s**'/ 'bed**s**'/ 'deserted'/ 'plantation**s**'/ 'rai**s**ed'/ 'voice**s**'):

in this ancestral land
there's an embryonic plant to be hoed
songs of September birds
rivers diverted from beds
deserted plantations
barbed wire circling raised voices

Regarding rhythm, French words tend to stress their last syllable, resulting in a higher percentage of French lines ending with stressed syllables than in English, as is the case for five of the six lines in the above example: 'ori**gine**', '**bêcher**', '**lit**', 'désert**ées**' and 's'é**lèvent**'. Four of the six end-line words in my translation also stress the last (and only) syllable: '**land**', '**hoed**', '**birds**' and '**beds**'. Mabanckou makes effective use of silence by inserting an extra space between the two stanzas of this poem—perhaps evoking the voices stifled by barbed wire in the last line of the first stanza.

In these three lines, Mabanckou is able to express his faith in the land, in the trees, and in humanity itself—the unifying refrain of this volume:

rester homme jusqu'au bout
tant que les arbres s'enracineront
dans la terre

remain human to the end
as long as trees take root
in the earth

I

WHEN THE ROOSTER ANNOUNCES THE DAWN OF ANOTHER DAY . . .

it's midnight
shrews and pangolins
already roam the banks
of the Loukoula
death is moaning in dens
thickets of silence
suddenly stir

my torch has gone out
I'm haunted by words
I can't wait to complete
this tale
before the break of day

now the eyes shut halfway
dreams are diverted
as soon as you drift off
towards the shores of that childhood
you lug around
like a shell scrubbed clean
by marine salts

borders go astray
I remember streams
manganese
Mayombe forest

Congo River
backbone of the homeland

you think you are writing
for relief
and you realize that words
incubate scars
of unfulfilled moments

the shadow precedes the hand
the extinguished light
finds the murmur again
of death-vigil nights

long is the distance
that's the only way
people can value
the path

don't forget
without birds
without trees
without rivers
no forest exists

how long
will sand keep the imprint
now that
in shadows
September winds blow

what will we have left

wind
the shadow of a land
the flutter of a day
lost 'in the swallow's beak'

we'll still have the dew
of a passionate morning
congealed sap
the shadows' song
in the screech owl's throat
the sneering of macaques
in banana fields

each day
each night
I learn about the share of guilt
buried in the ground

the dead look away
beyond the hills
giant silhouettes lie in wait for me
and demand atonement for crimes
committed by my own kind

how do I know that the wind
whispers the truth

how do I know that dead grass
doesn't collude with the drought

how do I know that death
clad in tattered clothes
no longer lurks behind enclosures

I blame my share of serenity
just as I blame my lack of tranquility
seeking in vain
a centre of gravity

I tell the wind to remove the stench
of rot
I tell the sun to illuminate
groves

I apologize
for the sake of the night
for the sake of those unable to speak
for the sake of carved-up lands

but there is the wound
the tree bark of the moment
the fatigue of its boughs
hope planted
at the start of a dried-up day

the wound that opens
the morning's taut skin
the swallow that hopes
to one day a summer make

a crimson river

cormorants with wounded wings
along the Coast
shells of snails in the sand
coconut palms bent
by winds

and so goes my homeland

I say ground cracks
roots dry up
seed no longer grows

I say space dwindles
roofs litter
the ground
roads lead
to culs-de-sac

I also say
I shoulder this cross

how many dreams
still drag their feet

childhood's so far away
nostalgia's ashes
cover the sleep of adults

some hungers can't be appeased

nation after nation
despair endures

longing for childhood knots the belly
territories spread
all over the surface
of memory

the signal comes from the hills
let's lay down our weapons
at the foot of the age-old tree

let's forget the blind resistance
being organized day and night
in lantana fields

barricades
traps on the village's threshold
troops on alert

the homeland's red soil
puts up with being defiled
by the soldiers' mob

I remember
our tight family ties
our entangled roots
our family tree
a succession of glorious ancestors

somewhere
words collapse
stone is proud of the silence
it protects

somewhere
clay decays
in the depths of the earth

thus rock becomes weak
and prehistoric geology's cycle
begins

one day History will be inscribed
on this forsaken tree
the nervures of its bark will intertwine
the streaming sap will overflow
down to its roots

and so mother
how to say those words
your words
the local dialect

the language of today
incubates poisoned assegais

god turns his back on us
night plunges us into the whirlwind
the hand that strikes
belongs to a brother

we share
forebears
the Kingdom
and funeral rites

you think you are writing
but time forces
the hand into motion
shadows blur sight
murmurs haunt hearing
till the mind
capitulates

there is nothing worse
than the grief of rônier palms
the sleep of swamps
the silence of passerines

there is nothing worse
than the gossip
of fire ants
praying mantis conventicles
agate eyes
in gloomy lairs
sky overcast with a wrinkled sheet

god turns his back on us

how to interpret
the tablet of laws
translate the portent
of night

for all was already transcribed

the space of a length of time
fits on a thin thread

distant calls
are only echoes
of captive words
words of the past
words effaced in caves

mother
night has since covered me
with its vastness

I've constructed a hut
with red earth
on the summit of exile
watching for suns
of this country confined by its shadow

don't listen

they've wounded the ventricles
of the homeland

shame is worn
like a party mask

who will say the name of the homeland
at the dawn of reconciliation

no voice is raised over here
they say the silence of plains
bodes well for attacks

victory
comes at the end of a gun
they say
conquest or death
they reprise

I tread on the glory
of their false martyrs
so I can pay my last respects
and bow my head
before this unknown corpse

I'm not to blame
said the migratory bird
I was gone for the winter
my only crime
is to sport the same
plumage as those in my branch

nonetheless
the birds of your kind
have sinned in your name

here comes
this nocturnal moment

here comes the shadow of first footprints
blue sand of the Coast
angels on alert
bursts of laughter
insouciance of dawns
with their lazy adornments

in memory of Amélia Néné, the poetess

here is the sea lauded by Loutard
death seated under the shade
of eucalyptus trees
by Mongo-Kamba graveyard
the plaint of the Palm-Lyre
whose leaves are plaited
by the Order of Phenomena
the Flowers of Life
wilted on the brink of a new day

a poetess died
the echo of her song is still warm

this suffering ghost
is U Tam'si who collects
in his hands
the crumbs of a land

here is also the moment
when despite itself
memory climbs back up
the craggy paths of the past
submerged in my veins
of a migratory bird

here are dazzling mornings
the dawn of seasons
the ripening of fields of corn
unspoiled spaces
the secret Realm
whose pylons collapse
with the first floods
of wandering

mother
here is a childhood like mine
an extinguished hearth
ashes at rest
the night ringed with uncertainties
the absence of a father's sceptre
no unruly brood
thrusting their hands
into the same bowl

here is this childhood
with bicycle hoops
old tyres from cars
slingshots
rubber sandals on feet
bare chests
short pants
secured by a wide strap

the road that led to school
behind buildings topped
with straw
hilliness
harsh terrain
at the end of which learning languished
from waiting so long

back then
the world was cramped
a few shacks
a block of clay huts
Les Bandas railway station
only one train each month
and borders barely extended beyond
the Loukoula's banks

from other lands
drum rolls
would reach our ears

here is a childhood that looks
like a clone of my own

the childhood that follows me
lone shadow stooped
from so much travelling on foot
the childhood that looks me
straight in the eyes
as night falls

here is the family plot of land
an enclosure made of bamboo
an orchard carpeted with dead leaves
a footpath that leads
to the Loukoula
livestock fighting their way
through the maze of lantanas
the grunts of hogs
in the mud

the childhood I bear
beyond the light

and the tree remembers
the news
the legend of wandering
on this Friday shrouded
in ash

the tree remembers
this legend

a grave
a cross
and a cloud of silence
ever since

.

in the shadow of your sleep
lie the remnants of dreams

months come and go
the dusts of seasons
cover the grief of that Friday
when the barn owl flew over the roof
announcing the news

they say the other horizon appears
beyond the hills

I don't beg the sun
for a sunbeam
I bear inside
the light of your awakening
the blinding light of your eyes
fixed on eternity

the house is half-crumbled
the roof destroyed
by the winds
but nighttime shadows look after
what's inside
the rafters resist termites
the fig tree thrives
soursop ripens in September
and grass grows again
with the first rains

one day the moon lodged a complaint
it was heard by the darkness

but the day erased the grievance of the moon

ever since
we have lost our memory

on Louboulou plain
a wild beast is in her death throes
an old hornless antelope
moist-eyed
with panting tongue
perhaps the silhouette
or an ancestor's double

what news will come
from the Loukoula's opposite shore?

mother
now I hear the oracle
murmur your final words

'this is my last will and testament
written in the shade of silence
not far from the meadow
of death
at the hour when the weary camel
quickens its pace
to reach the oasis . . .

'this is my last will and testament
dying wishes wrested
from the night
to read when the common cranes
take wing
before the rooster proclaims
the dawn of another day . . .

'my dying wishes
words to translate for the deaf
not for the deaf who hear
the voices of silence
but for the deaf who don't want
to hear . . .

'this is my last will and testament
I Kengué daughter of Moukila
born in Louboulou
distant ochre lands
yellow and burnt
savannahs hills fords
slash-and-burn lands
of tubers and antelopes

'this is my last will and testament

not knowing how to read
or write
I sign this with an x
and speak in my own voice
through the trance I breathe
into the scribe that you see here

'this is my last will and testament
I don't know from where this conflict comes
but beware of the sky
in retreat
none of you will be able to read
the whispering of ancestors
on the faces of masks
if in each corner of a hut
I catch sight of the glare
of a gun'

II

AS LONG AS TREES TAKE ROOT
IN THE EARTH

I sell to the other century
the erring ways of my serpentine fate
I lay claim to my two-faced
identity split with time

I shred here and now
the birth record of borders
to baptize the new expanse to be won

shame on you for restricting me
to this plot of land
and handing me a tom-tom to beat

so take your hollowed-out Negritude
carry it like a viaticum
make sure you don't forget your assegai
let alone your woven mat
they expect you like this
clad in leopard skin

my only bonds
are the sum of all intersections
the echoes of Babel

here is my flagpole in the heart of a new land
adoption binds me with buried roots
deep within this existence being built one day at a time

keep your meaningless truth
speak for the Master
and betray my land
for a modest sum
that's what they expect of you

I adopt from the bird
uncertainty about the next bush

I don't know what the weather will bring
on migration's other side
but the world opens to me
rich in crossroads

let my wings carry me
carry me further away from the hue and cry
away from the barn
away from the cocks trained to fight

don't change your name
don't change your branch
remain human until the end
as long as trees take root
in the earth

every second
the dream of this distant horizon
the homeland returned in the cycle of seasons
the crack in this blue that's bruised
but always renewed

carry inside yourself the expanse of bewildered azure
the shred of hope disappeared on a heron's wings
the spark of a dawning day
in the trough of a wave of delusions

in this ancestral land
there's an embryonic plant to be dug up
songs of September birds
rivers diverted from beds
deserted plantations
barbed wire circling raised voices

remain human until the end
as long as trees take root
in the earth

there's more to say about a grain of sand
than an elephant

freedom is on this side
make no mistake about it

the other world is the last of utopias
standing amidst the winds
here Paradise reaches its end

life's a contingency

beaten down by so many white seasons
I'll succumb one day
I know it

but someplace there'll be a tree
the same that moved its branches in my poems
a rônier palm with leaves turning brown
whose sap will freely flow

I'll sleep beside my dreams
my childhood will melt in the morning mist
my spirit will follow the trampling of herds
a swallow will take to the air
carefully grazing the family plot
my mother's shape will emerge at last from the gloom

what shadow comes once more
to tarnish the serene sky
on this day when the swift
begins to sing of reconciliation

I tell the wind
to toss dead leaves
to bend filao boughs
to wring the gown of the heavenly vault
to muffle the moans of rock

here the contours of this land fade
darkness and night intertwine
in a harmony wounding the flora
some remnants of suns hang
from fig tree limbs

autochtons henceforth
turn their gaze towards the clumps of clouds that have
swallowed for ever
what was left for us of the sky's azure

this is the land where the dead come back to life
by the sea

the land where trees shed tears too

our spent tomorrows

the legend of our wanderings

here's where the tree will tell us
the depth of the ground
the rooting of our dreams
the muffling of our dead
since the composting of ages
down to the dawns of used-up days

the fruit of remorse is so sour
it's no longer enough to blame the rain
the savannahs' dryness
the echo of gourds hanging in doorways
near earthenware water jugs
aluminium cooking pots
wooden spoons

does the man who takes shelter beneath the tree
measure the patience of bark
the steady labour of roots
the resistance of humus

and now the wind also speaks
the leaves fly away
proclaiming the news

the current sweeps them along
in the swirl of the falls

in this desert you don't need much
a ray of sun
so that silent intonations of nature
ascend
the mirage of vowels
the alchemy of toppled consonants

to the loss of flora
we must add the species trampled by cattle
the traps no longer catching eels
the sneezing of arid soil
the dens where skeletal wild beasts dwell

who can resent the migratory bird
for rising above its nest

don't change your name
don't change your branch

remain human until the end
as long as trees take root
in the earth

the umbilical cord's agreement
only is binding to barnyard birds
those who delimit horizons
to the village's furthest abodes

one day we'll read on the crypt
the last requests of the free man
a white dove will fly over our disbelief

then who will give voice
to the song of Redemption

walking gnaws at shoes
years peel away under the sole
of persistence

little by little the call from within subsides
while other paths open
for taking or leaving behind

that day will come
when we'll finally know
that angels have no wings
except those hoisting human imagination towards manic heights

eyes open to everyday glow
it will be up to us to construct tomorrow's tale
the one we'll tell those who believe that angels have wings

draw your strength from the lifeless leaf
break all bonds until you can tie your fate
to the baobab trunk

don't hold within yourself any discounted dream
on the public square
don't look at the will-o'-the-wisp
constantly climb back up the slope
even if steep
the voices arriving from the other hill
are only echoes

here's where the source of origins flowed
drought has eroded the flint
no knife blade remembers
the hunters passing through

it's up to the wind to narrate the traces again

here comes the time of hypocritical laughter
the time of mediocrity served at every turn
the time when humans no longer descend from the apes
but regress
the time of peddlers of pipe dreams
the time of fake wizards

here comes the rule of men draped in deceit
modern-day Sisyphuses lug rancour
like doomsday ladybugs
sentenced to rolling the shit to the next riverbank

now the malicious word burdened by noxious seed
grows on our future's innocence

beware the gleam of dawn
that fateful moment when masks will fall
and we will see colonies of hares
with pricked up ears

the false prophets summon Diop
whom they haven't read

the false prophets summon Fanon
whom they haven't read

the false prophets summon Césaire
whom they haven't read

so here is the haughty mountain
proud of its height

here is the mountain of the soul
silent keeper of boundlessness

here is the mountain that hasn't spoken in centuries
it only asks for a bit of blue sky
grass forever green
morning dew
a herd grazing close by
all kinds of birds
that sing

let's ask the stone where to find Truth
it will tell us it's in this earthly world
and only here

it's in this earthly world where wind stirs
oceans twist and turn
waterways split

it's in this earthly world where dreams straddle borders

pierce invisible walls

and Humankind has claimed to be the superior species
since time began
while day after day the tree laughs at this belief

extracts its wisdom's nectar
from the depths of the earth
swings its branches to signal Victory

remain human until the end
as long as trees take root in the earth

AN OPEN LETTER TO
THOSE WHO ARE KILLING POETRY

We've heard it all before: the audience for poetry has dissipated. A conclusion reached almost in a burst of apocalyptic unanimity. Must we resign ourselves, throw in the towel, sing the same old tune of a 'chronicle of a death foretold'? There would be nothing left for us to do but let the infernal machine inevitably run its course. Nothing left for us except to compose the eulogy in alexandrines and rich rhymes, solemnly make arrangements for the funeral, find a vast graveyard somewhere by the sea, and draft an epitaph with the following words:

Here lies Dame Poetry, idolized by Ronsard,
Hugo, U Tam'si and the others, forsaken by
ungrateful and profligate heirs . . .

Poetry, last rampart of the soul in all its profundity, may thus be at death's door. This bedridden dowager, for whom all surgical interventions have failed, is still surrounded by a few diehard devotees who cling to her until the final breath. Just as the poet Abdellatif Laâbi speaks of the 'dying Sun', poetry is dying, and as a consequence, we may be guilty of one of the most shameful infractions of the penal code: failure to render assistance to an endangered person—I was going to say, *to endangered poetry* . . .

Nowadays, writing or publishing poetry seems an act of resistance, like sporting a mohawk. The space devoted to poetry has eroded over time. And so poets, from the refuge of their islets, look at this world that has turned its back on them and wonder from where this disaffection arose.

Did the prevailing confusion, the temptation of mediocrity, end up stacking the deck? Unless it's the very definition of poetry that's at stake? But can we define a notion that lends itself to the real world, rather than to the realm of conjecture?

Pedestrian Poems and Inspired Poems

It's true that the malaise is real. We can't hide this frightening reality. Even so, who among us, readers and poets, wonders what caused the dethroning of poetry? We console ourselves, especially the poets, believing that better times will soon return when poetry will be restored to its former glory. When that day comes, the novel had better watch out. What arguments haven't we heard to that effect? We are told the novel has never been as prominent as it is today. It was once, if I may be so bold as to oversimplify, a means to put food on the table, was serialized in the daily papers and eventually published in traditional book form. Poetry was then the preferred discipline, the genre of seduction, enchantment, etiquette and emotion.

We take comfort where we can.

Many observers blame the Surrealists for creating poetry's current malaise. Apparently, they drove away the audience for this literary genre by imposing knee-jerk and unconscious automatic writing, thereby forsaking music, emotion—the very quintessence of poetry. Form may have killed substance, but who cares about substance as long as there's form!

We forget that traditional poetry, without denigrating it, was hampered by a proliferation of rules that reduced the poet to a counter of syllables, a scout for beautiful alexandrines.

We came up with perfect stanzas, verses that were accurate and flawless in prosody. But they had to be *inspired*. Here, I believe, lies the main reason for the divorce between poetry and its readers. There's a strident difference between a *pedestrian poem* and an *inspired poem*. The former originates from humans, and solely from humans. Admittedly, the latter originates from humans as well, but they feel they are serving as intermediaries, scribes, couriers. It is poetry, the kind that simultaneously belongs to and is able to dissociate itself from humankind, that keeps its virginity and watches the years go by without losing its substance.

Pedestrian poetry is what Annie Lebrun rightly describes as language poetry. She believes that such poetry, 'being only worth its weight in paper, discourages us a little more each day from still banking on words.'

That's why it's not surprising to hear it said that poetry is not what it used to be. There are no longer any rhymes. The writing is unreadable. What do they want to say?

Why Write Poetry?
What Function Can It Fulfil?

Judging from a few contemporary publications, I realize that assigning a function to poetry is not so easy. Each poet sounds the alarm in their own way. Reading between the lines, we quickly detect despair, pessimism. Take, for example, Belgian poet Gaspard Hons, for whom poetry is a 'blade of grass that thrives despite a scant amount of water'. There's a touch of resistance and much resignation in this definition. The grass may thrive despite 'this scant amount of water'. In other words, in spite of the shortage of water, poetry is here, settling for whatever cramped space is left.

On the other hand, Cuban poet Eliseo Diego's viewpoint is less extreme, though it conveys a certain sense of withdrawal:

A poem is nothing but happiness, a conversation in twilight,
all that's gone and was replaced by silence.

This perspective reminds me of Polish poet Julian Tuwim, who nevertheless broadens the discussion when he asserts:

> When I know that the poem will be, I enclose the universe within parentheses, and I place the sign of the function upfront.

It should be noted that Tuwim corroborates what was pointed out apropos of the *inspired poem*. Poetry comes before its function. The question of its utility, of its role, comes later. The fundamental mistake some poets make is asking about the function of poetry before even questioning the process of creation and the way poetry gushes out uncontrollably. These poets, of whom there are many nowadays, confuse the battle cry with the poem. As passionate propagandists, former trade unionists, experts on conflicts that give them something to sink their teeth into, mediocre self-proclaimed lawyers for war victims, or incorrigible nationalists, they embrace all causes. Incapable of producing a piece of writing worth its salt, they pretend to be the protectors of purity and authenticity, and cultivate intolerance instead of taming their acrimony and envy. And then, what to tell them? At least have mercy on them, grant them the words they long to hear, the status of writer that they claim. As far as I'm concerned, I embrace the wisdom of Albert Cohen in *Book of My Mother*:

> I have resolved to tell all the painters they are geniuses; otherwise they bite. And, in general, I tell each one they are charming. Such are my daytime manners. But in my nights and my dawns, my thoughts are not constrained.

Why Poetry Anthologies Are Nothing but Rip-Offs

A few African authors have lately been churning out a kind of facile poetry. Hamidou Dia, a former contributor to *Présence Africaine*, may well be their brilliant and energetic leader. It's always quite an honour to be a leader. We must beware of not leading the flock into the abyss of mediocrity! Reading the lines from this 'pan-African' school, you are dumbfounded. For these upstanding people, there are, on the one hand, the 'good Blacks' who champion good Black African poetry; and on the other, the sellouts: those who consort with the Whites, crisscross book fairs, savour champagne and petits fours. So one must close ranks, call in the genuine Black poets, round them up to bellow in unison, praise Césaire, Damas and Senghor, even without having read them—it doesn't matter! And Hamidou Dia has produced for us an anthology entitled *Poètes d'Afrique et des Antilles,* published by Éditions de la Table Ronde, in order to replicate what Senghor had done in his day with his celebrated *Anthologie de la poésie nègre.* The back cover of Hamidou Dia's book speaks for itself once you know that authors often write these blurbs themselves, and the one below probably fell prey to such an exercise in conceitedness:

> No new anthology of African poetry has been published since Senghor's, and yet the creativity of francophone poets is considerable. Hence this writers' anthology conceived by Hamidou Dia, a poet of renown and an academic. His anthology is intended for the general public and traces the evolution of African poetry from the Negritude movement to the intimism that characterizes contemporary poetry, including the emergence of a new feminine lyricism. Hamidou Dia was born in Senegal. He studied in Saint Louis and Dakar, and was imprisoned for political dissidence. He earned a French literature teacher certification, and teaches at the University of Cergy-Pontoise. He has published numerous poetry collections with *Présence Africaine.*

So we are informed that Hamidou Dia is the reputed successor of Senghor on the subject. We also learn that he has published 'numerous poetry collections', that he is a poet 'of renown'. Browsing through the catalogue of *Présence Africaine*, I found no more than two poetry collections published under the name of Hamidou Dia. Poet of renown? If he says so, let's believe him—he knows his own worth!

What strikes me is that Senghor brought attention to poets who later became established authors, such as the Guadeloupean Guy Tirolien, while our 'poet of renown', Hamidou Dia, sets out to erase and truncate, shamelessly wielding the scissors of censorship. How else can we explain that this anthology ignores the voices of today's essential authors, such as Nimrod from Chad, Abdourahman A. Waberi from Djibouti, Labou Tansi and Gabriel Okoundji from the Congo and so many others?

One may argue that I am resentful because I myself did not make the list. Good grief! That's not the question. What I am condemning is all this demagoguery that hints of Stalinism. In the end, confusing the act of creation with blind obedience can only hurt poetry. Most of the poets excluded from this anthology are those who refuse to bleat in unison and transform creation into a federation of griots, epigones and pale imitations of the bards of Negritude. These free-spirited poets know you can't sing *Le cahier d'un retour au pays* a second time, so they let the singularity of their voices be heard, all the while acknowledging their kinship to Negritude. Is it a coincidence if one of the finest monographs about Senghor—Nimrod's *Le tombeau de Léopold Sédar Senghor* (Éditions Le Temps qu'il fait)—was just published by one of the poets brushed aside from this partisan anthology?

Let's return instead to the genuine poets, the genuine writers. Tuwim recognizes that the poem *must come*, but he *doesn't know* when. Then what to think of poets who write to order on such and such a topic: hunger, Rwanda, civil wars? Is this really creation? Creators must have doubts about everything. Their abilities to outdo themselves. Inspiration. Will it or won't it come, if ever? I don't mean to say that the literature of urgency is a bad thing in itself. Some writings are timeless. I'm thinking of Victor Hugo's *Les Châtiments* or Aimé Césaire's *Le cahier d'un retour au pays natal*. But not everyone is a Victor Hugo. Not everyone is an Aimé Césaire.

What about the poetry of urgency? A number of African poets have grasped this nuance. For them, poetry shouldn't lose its social function. Indeed, Babacar Sall writes: 'Everything must be precise / death / charity / good works / philanthropy / crime / also the word must be precise like a knife.' This literature of urgency is often tied to the poet's personal journey. How many of these 'militant' poets have a personal journey? It's only at this price that poetry avoids the pitfalls of writing on command, of writing poetry that is perfunctory, soulless and devoid of genuine feeling. Thus, we have heard some writers calling on their colleagues to 'take care' of AIDS, to fight the disease through their writing. In any case such was the opinion of Malagasy writer Michèle Rakotoson at the New Congress of Writers from Africa and the African Diaspora held in N'Djamena in October 2003. Next, they'll also call on writers to fight cancer, sleeping sickness or multiple sclerosis! The writer is nothing more than the firefighter of African societies.

Is poetry only to be an accumulation of words? No, according to Ivorian writer Tanella Boni: 'Words no longer make sense / Murdered / Gutted . . . ' Poets are aware of the ambiguity of words. They also invoke imagery and natural elements to define creation. Fernando d'Almeida, a Cameroonian poet, believes there will be poetry as long as 'trees still root in the earth'. Paul Dakeyo, another Cameroonian poet, whose early work was very militant, later turned to the natural elements that only women are meant to master: 'I dream about this river that is my land, and where currents drink up the sun that gushes from the highest peaks.' Finally, for Congolese poet Jean-Baptiste Tati-Loutard: 'The poet navigates between sky and earth like a sentient object between the two poles of a magnet.'

The Novel Comes to the Rescue of Poetry

No, poetry is not dead. It is sitting somewhere, ruefully watching the indifferent passers-by. In fact, we must fetch poetry from wherever it has retreated. Poetry is no longer the prerogative of leaflets or collections. Many real-life stories, short stories and novels perpetuate the poetic tradition. A few novels by writers from the new generation come to mind, such as Gaston-Paul Effa of Cameroon, whose pages are undeniably poetic. The first sentence of his novel *Mâ* would make any poet turn green with envy:

> Shadows have fallen, it's already night, in the network of alleyways on the seven hills of Yaoundé, at the end of the world, at the end of the sky and, on the sharp edge of the moon, I, Sabeth, am weeping.

Jean-Luc Raharimanana, a Malagasy writer, is 'wrongly' introduced as an author of short stories. His writings are pages of poetry whose lyrical brilliance baffles those who expect him to narrate a story in a straightforward way:

> And the night sets in, dark hole in the day. And the day
> sinks into the hole of the night, a spiral, succumbs there.
> Here comes the darkness . . .

The novels by Haitian Louis-Philippe Dalembert, in a formal and unique register, evoke his homeland, sea crossings, exile. So too do the prose pieces by Djiboutian author Waberi, who incidentally confesses:

> I am, in fact, a trafficker. I write poetry, but as it doesn't sell, I
> dress it up like a novel . . .

Clearly, most of the novelists mentioned above nurture strong ties with poetry. Waberi talks about 'making it look like a novel' to better 'sell'. For all these poets who have developed a reputation as prose writers, poetry has become a secret island from which gush themes they later develop in their novels, real-life stories or short stories. I am tempted to say: If you want to read poetry, read certain novels instead.

So Goes Poetry

Perhaps poetry, far from being at death's door, has only found a refuge. It has vacated its usual stomping grounds to follow in the footsteps of its heralds. There's no point in snivelling, in bemoaning the bygone days of lyrical flights and declamations, when we made the beloved blubber from the tight embrace of enclosed rhymes. Poetry has a new look. It has turned into thematically organized storytelling which no poet will be able to escape any longer. It accompanies prose, takes it by the hand, seduces it, makes it solemn, profound, sinuous but virulent, so it can emerge from the morass in which the contemporary novel has gotten itself mired. Where some praise the orality of a passage, its philosophical dimension, I see true poetry—the kind that restores to writing its turmoil, its edginess—ingredients necessary for a successful work.

But why do we no longer read poetry? Wrong question! Is what is presented to us really poetry? That's the question! Any piece of writing that dishes up free verse and freedom from rules now passes for poetry. We must join forces against such alarming permissiveness. Not that we demand the return of versification but we expect that poets write *inspired* texts, unlike the cerebral impudence so dear to Denis Roche and his group of poets and friends who stabbed in broad daylight, in the public square, the last modicum of human language: poetry. Since then, poetry, covered in bandages, has been walking with a limp and suffers from a slew of other ailments: editorial cronyism, the proliferation of self-publishing, the lack of interest from booksellers and the media. Cronyism is the most widespread abuse in the Parisian editorial microcosm. Poetry collections—if any still exist—from Seuil,

Gallimard or Flammarion, only publish their friends or the latest celebrities—Houellebecq, Roubaud and members of the French academy who empty the bottoms of drawers to make public their dusty verses about their teenage loves.

At the same time, francophone poetry has never been as prolific but lacking in recognition: Abdellatif Laâbi, Tahar Bekri, Tati-Loutard, Edouard Maunick, Jacques Rabemananjara, René Depestre, Jean Métellus, Nimrod, Gabriel Okoundji, among others.

And so goes poetry.

Translator's Notes

PAGE 9

'In the swallow's beak' alludes to a line from Jacques Prévert's poem *Les mystères de la chambre noire* [The Mysteries of the Darkroom].

PAGE 38

Amélia Néné (1954–1996) was a Congolese poet whose first book was titled *Fleurs de vie*. She was married to Congolese politician and poet Jean-Baptiste Tati-Loutard (1938–2009), who wrote *Le Palmier-Lyre* and *L'Ordre des phénomènes*.

PAGE 39

Tchicaya U Tam'si, pseudonym of Gérald Félix Tchicaya (1931–1988), was a Congolese French-language writer and poet.

Translator's Acknowledgements

I am grateful beyond words for Catherine Maigret Kellogg's invaluable contribution to polishing the early draft of this manuscript. In addition, my unbounded gratitude goes to my husband, Ted Miller, for believing in this project and facilitating my meeting with Alain Mabanckou in Los Angeles, right before the pandemic hit. Additionally, I am indebted to the editorial team at Seagull Books, for bringing this collection into the world: Naveen Kishore, at the helm, along with Sunandini Banerjee, Sayoni Ghosh and Bishan Samaddar.

★

Many thanks to the editors of the following literary journals in which versions of these translations first appeared:

Asymptote: 'An Open Letter to Those Who Are Killing Poetry'

The Cincinnati Review: 'here's where the tree will tell us', 'the house is half-crumbled', 'the signal comes from the hills'

The Georgia Review: 'and so mother', 'don't change your name', 'here the contours', 'here's where the source of origins', 'the space of a length of time', 'the tree remembers'

Guernica: 'in this ancestral land'

Harvard Review (Omniglots): 'and now the wind also speaks', 'on Louboulou plain', 'there's more to say'

Mentor & Muse: Essays from Poets to Poets: 'god turns his back on us/ night', 'here comes the rule of men', 'in this ancestral land'

The Michigan Quarterly Review: 'does the man who takes shelter', 'god turns his back on us/ night', 'god turns his back on us/ how', 'here comes the rule of men', 'how many dreams', 'I'm not to blame', 'in this desert', 'it's midnight', 'I sell to the other century', 'mother', 'there's nothing worse/ than the gossip'

Pleiades: 'beaten down by so many seasons', 'shame on you', 'the umbilical cord's agreement'

Prairie Schooner: 'the false prophets summon Diop', 'now the malicious word'

Puerto del Sol: 'back then', 'borders go astray', 'here is also the moment', 'here is the family plot of land', 'here is this childhood', 'mother', 'we'll still have the dew'

Two Lines: 'I adopt from the bird', 'to the loss of flora', 'what shadow comes once more'

Waxwing: 'mother/ now I hear the oracle', 'one day the moon lodged a complaint', 'somewhere/ clay'

World Literature Today: 'draw your strength', 'let's ask the stone'